M000191651

Part-memoir, part-lexicon, this artful inquisition of the terminology surrounding adoption took my breath away. Fierce and eloquent, Karen Pickell handles the delicate material of her own life with searing honesty and precision, while simultaneously calling out the grief, loss, and sense of abandonment that is the reality of adoption. I wish I could have had this beautiful book as my companion and guide as I fought to navigate the anguish and complexities of my own adopted life. *An Adoptee Lexicon* is a gift; a must-read for anyone touched by adoption, a triumph of love over loss, and a powerful and searing reminder of the redemptive power of truth. **—Caitríona Palmer, author of *An Affair with My Mother* (Penguin Ireland)**

In *An Adoptee Lexicon*, Karen Pickell divines not only the terminology of adoption, but words so often taken for granted—sin, child, name, parent, home—in the formation of all our identities, cutting through clichés that impede self-actualization and empathy. That we might not know who we truly are—that we might be wandering "detached from the earth itself, from the world of living things," as Pickell hauntingly writes—is a truth this book embraces and with which it struggles, in which any reader, regardless of family history, can find kinship.

Whether unpacking the myriad forms of legal, medical, and sociopolitical literature on adoption and related issues or depicting moments of personal anguish and loss with visceral, necessary honesty, Pickell relates, through poetic narrative and stirring exposition, that wholeness is not some end-all, be-all goal but a process of truly seeing and loving our fragmented selves. In one of my favorite parables, told by the Sufi mystic Attar, a group of birds goes off seeking God and instead finds a mirror. *An Adoptee Lexicon* is a mirror like this. That we have the chance to hold it to our own faces—particularly as citizens inhabiting a moment in which we all, in our woundedness, are urgently needed—is a challenge and a blessing, expressed in the way its author comes from "blood and paperwork," the way she is "drawn to water, walks through trees," the way, though some tried to make it so, she did not disappear. **—Christopher Martin, 2018 Georgia Author of the Year in Memoir for *This Gladdening Light* (Mercer University Press)**

Adoptee perspectives are rare treasures in the adoption sector. Karen's insights on common frequently used terms offer a vulnerable glimpse of how these terms impact those who they were intended to help. This text should be read by anyone who frequently utters any of these significant phrases! **—Angela Tucker, founder of The Adopted Life LLC and director of post-adoption services at Amara**

Karen is a gifted writer. This may be her first book, but it certainly won't be her last. She has used her extensive talent to provide the voice that is most overlooked in the adoption narrative, that of the adopted individual.

Successful marketing has created a false narrative of adoption. Brokers facilitating adoption don't focus on the barbaric pain that lasts a lifetime. Instead, the billion-dollar adoption industry has institutionalized the term "proper adoption language," which frames adoption through the prism of eager parents. Karen eloquently reveals the impact of "proper adoption language" on those who are at the center of adoption—adoptees. Using her phenomenal writing skill, she brings the reader to inhabit her being. Karen promulgates how the powerful adoption industry's words have shaped adoption while ignoring the voice of the adoptee. **—Leslie Pate Mackinnon, LCSW, educator, activist, and Baby Scoop Era mother**

An Adoptee Lexicon should be read by every adoptee who has ever felt alone. Though many adoptees try not to dwell on it, we also have the space inside of us Karen so aptly describes. Her work speaks to our often ambiguous reality: fit or misfit, embraced or denied, secret or light. We choose to channel our energy related to angst, hurt, and feelings of being misunderstood in a variety of ways. That Karen has chosen to channel hers into writing and self-expression is our fortune. *An Adoptee Lexicon* is soul baring, transparent, and risky—what many adoptive or birth parents won't want to read, but should understand. **—Betsie Norris, founder/ executive director of Adoption Network Cleveland: The Ohio Family Connection and adoptee**

Karen offers an insightful and penetrating window into the adoptee experience through her selection and exposition of the charged language in adoption. Adoptees: read this and feel understood. Others: read this to understand the triggering language that permeates the adoption space. **—Haley Radke, creator and host of the podcast Adoptees On**

AN ADOPTEE LEXICON

Karen Pickell

Raised Voice Press

Clearwater, Florida

Copyright © 2018 by Karen Pickell

Published by Raised Voice Press
PO Box 14502
Clearwater, Florida 33766
www.raisedvoicepress.com

All rights reserved. No part of this book may be reproduced without the publisher's written permission, except for brief quotations in reviews.

Cover photo by Daniel Fazio on Unsplash
Cover and interior design by Karen Pickell

Published in the United States of America

ISBN 978-1-949259-00-1 (Paperback)
ISBN 978-1-949259-01-8 (Ebook–Kindle)
ISBN 978-1-949259-02-5 (Ebook–EPUB)

Library of Congress Control Number: 2018951260

For Brian and Kayla
and all descendants of
the girls sent away and the boys unconsidered

AN ADOPTEE LEXICON

SIN

In the beginning was original sin, and it was the woman's fault: Eve, tempted by the snake. But didn't the snake do the tempting in the first place? Where was Adam while this was going on?

When I learned about original sin, I felt the weight of blame for the temptation my body held for boys and men, all those impure thoughts the nuns and priests talked about. My fault for wearing the uniform skirt I was required to wear.

Girls at my single-sex Catholic high school who got pregnant (and discovered) disappeared. I guessed they were expelled. Their accomplices at the boys' schools graduated on time, no one the wiser.

> At the time a student becomes aware of parental responsibilities, s/he or the family must notify the school. Meetings will be scheduled with the student(s), parents, school counselor, and the principal to discuss the educational options available to the student(s). Marian Catholic will make every effort to permit the student(s) to continue class work. Regular classroom attendance and participation in extra-curricular activities will be based on the health, safety, and well-being of the student and the child, as well as the best interests of the school community. (*2015–16 Student Handbook,* Marian Catholic High School [Chicago Heights, IL])

> When RJHS becomes aware of the pregnancy of a student or the impending fatherhood of a student, the Counseling Department will schedule a conference with the student, the

student's parent(s)/guardian(s), school counselor and a representative of the school administration. In the exercise of its sole discretion, the school will determine the appropriate course of action for meeting the student's educational goals. (*2017–18 Student Handbook,* Regis Jesuit High School [Aurora, CO])

Acts of premarital sex are serious sins. When sexual misconduct results in pregnancy, the school's response reaffirms its respect for the sanctity of all human life. While the charity of Christ moves us to forgive and help a young woman and a young man when a pregnancy results, in no way should our commitment to respond to the priority of life be interpreted as ignoring, treating lightly or condoning sexual misconduct. . . . Any student pregnancy requires a careful analysis of the student's current status and presents the possibility of unique circumstances that require consideration. The KMC administration has the responsibility for considering the specific circumstances regarding any pregnancy and determining the parties' future attendance at the school. (*2017–18 Student Handbook,* Kapaun Mt. Carmel Catholic High School [Wichita, KS])

Instead of high school, my mother graduated from beauty school. She didn't even get to keep me as a consolation prize. I remember reading *The Scarlet Letter* in high school and thinking of her, before I knew her. I always knew I was born from sin.

The priest who wedded my pregnant cousin to her unborn child's father used the occasion to pontificate on the symbolism of a white wedding dress. The groom wore black, which wasn't mentioned.

My son, born before his father and I were married, was conceived from love, from wishes I made upon stars twinkling above a great lake. Mother was all I ever wanted to be. If this offends anyone, I'm not sorry.

BABY

The other day my mother talked about "the baby," how her torment over the baby never ends, never goes away, how the baby is thrown in her face still, today, and don't I see what she deals with?

In this conversation, I am "the baby," yet I am not the baby she imagines. I am a nearly fifty-year-old woman. The baby has her own babies, who aren't at all babies either. The baby thinks her own thoughts and speaks them aloud. The baby has a name, and it is not the name her mother gave her. The baby was rehomed, recertified. The baby has a driver's license and a passport that prove she is living a separate life under a different name than the baby my mother remembers.

When I had my first baby, I was terrified someone would try to take him from me. My husband and I were not yet married, and even though he was at the hospital with me, the staff treated me like a single mother, and in my chest there was a weight that grew heavier the longer I was there, a fear that I would not be allowed to leave the hospital with my baby. I had not spent a night in a hospital since the nights I spent in a hospital nursery after I was born. After that first hospital stay, I left with a stranger who took me to a baby home, an orphanage of sorts, to await adoption.

My mother once insisted she was alone when she gave birth to me. I said, No, I was there, too. I was with her. She became furious, yelled at me that NO, I wasn't there, SHE WAS ALONE. I am not the baby she remembers. The baby is not a person at all, only a thing that once caused her pain, that continues to cause her pain today.

I did not cause her pain. I was the baby. I was helpless, crying for her, wanting to be where I could smell her, wanting to drink her milk.

The night after my second baby was born, they took her to the nursery. After too long a time had passed, I called and told them to bring her back. I waited, but they didn't bring her. I called again. Then I heard crying coming down the hall, coming closer, and I recognized it was my daughter. They brought her in, and she was crying so furiously she couldn't be calmed. The nurse put her in my arms, and she screamed. The nurse took her back from me and bounced her until the crying quieted. I took her back and thought, Never again will they take her to the nursery. She will stay beside me, in my room, and I will be the one who calms her when she cries.

NAME

A word or phrase that constitutes the distinctive designation of a person or thing.

Distinguishes one from another, one from many. Identifies. Relates.

There is a set of names I can choose from:

Given name 1, a gift from my mother.

Middle name 1, same as middle name 2.

Surname 1, assigned at my birth.

Surname never given (call it surname 1b, or maybe surname 0), not allowed at my birth, permission not having been granted.

Given and surname 2, my renaming.

Confirmation name, chosen by me, forgotten by all after the ceremony's end.

Surname 3, available to me after marrying the person with whom I chose to form a family.

We are free to choose any name we please. All one must do is file some paperwork in their state of residence. I could choose a name no one gave me. I could flip open a White Pages, close my eyes, put my finger down, and use whatever name it lands on as my own.

My ancestors' names were bungled and distorted and Americanized during their early years in the United States. Surname spellings were altered, given names were recorded incorrectly on forms. I want to tell them to fight harder to keep their names. Don't they understand what a name means? I wish they had thought of the possibility of me, a hundred years later, searching for something solid to hold.

A word or symbol used in logic to designate an entity.

My mother hates my name. She prefers to call me by the name she gave me. During those first months after I found her, I allowed this renaming. I began to call myself Kimberly when interacting with her and my sister. I felt the split down my middle growing wider. I felt my life sorting into nested befores and afters. I considered legally changing my name, again. I thought of combining all my names somehow into one long descriptive phrase.

Another term for surname is family name. With every surname comes a family.

Many adopted people do not know their own families' surnames. They cannot be sure of where in the world their people live. They cannot be sure of their own ancestry or, in some cases, ethnicity.

Knowing your own name is power. It is being able to look at a map and point to the place on earth where your people originated. It is being able to say exactly who you are, or were.

I think of myself as both Kimberly and Karen. I think of myself as a member of four families, one for each surname I claim. But I use the name that binds me to the family I created, the people who are wholly mine. I have identified myself.

FAMILY TREE

Is family a tree? Is a tree anything at all like my family? From what seed did my family tree grow? A tree once upon a time did not exist. Or, a tree can be traced back to the very first tree of its kind, back to the very first tree on earth. What does this matter, though, to a tree? The seed of my family was the longing I had to be connected to other human beings. The seed was a moment beside an office elevator when I was introduced to a man I would later marry. The seed was a couple of teenagers fooling around. The seed was the handoff of a baby to strangers. Where do the roots of one family end and those of another family begin? My tree is a live oak, gnarled, twisted, slow growing but sturdy, up to the challenge of time, content to host hangers-on—moss, worms, squirrels. My family is the people I love, the people who matter to me, and the people they love, the people who matter to them. My family is blood and paperwork. I am the trunk of my family tree. My roots are deeper than they appear. My arms are spread wide and able to support the weight of other bodies, other hearts. My family is a forest with roots entwined beneath the surface, with new trees sprouting all the time, nourished by the remains of elders that have fallen.

NATIVE

To be of the place where one was born. To reside in that place. To be from that place. To originate there.

How to be native to any place when you feel as though you were never born from another human being, when you feel as though you originated from a transaction. When you feel detached from the earth itself, from the world of living things. Alien. Foreign.

I have not seen the building I was born in or the building where I lived during the first three months of my life. The woman whose body I grew inside has no stories to tell me of how I moved in her belly. I originated from lust, from loneliness.

I am native to my mother's body, native to someplace in Cleveland where two drunk kids barely copulated. I am native to the city in which I was raised, yet I feel detached from it, as if it cannot be mine because everything I know of it belongs to my adoptive family.

I am native to this skin that contains me, these bones that hold me up, this mind that never rests, these hands, these feet. I am native to this heart.

CHILD

A child does not own her life, except for what she keeps to herself, her interior world, and those moments when she is able to move unattended by adults in the exterior world. A child's life is dictated by parents and teachers and pastors. They decide what's best for her, where and how and with whom she should live. They decide the name she will have, the language she'll speak, the customs she'll learn. They decide whom she'll be instructed to love, to whom she'll be required to pledge loyalty. They tell her how to behave, what to say or to not ever say, what is allowed and what is forbidden. A child has only small choices available to her, decisions insignificant to everyone else: whom to dream about, how to imagine the future, what to share and what to keep for herself. To behave as expected or to not give a shit. To do one while seeming to do the other. Whom to actually love or not.

No child can ever be kept. They all leave. They choose their own lives and their own loves. She who cannot leave childhood behind is trapped, always small yet wearing an adult façade. Growing up is moving on, letting go, getting real. There is a need to reconcile childhood somehow, to understand it with one's adult mind. But to rehash the past, over and over and over, with no revelation, no insight, no figuring out, is to relive it the way a soldier relives a battle after returning home. A nightmare you can't escape. A horror movie that never stops playing. Over and over and over. Bodies break down trying to outrun the past on a treadmill.

PLACEMENT

My placement with my adoptive family was based on their desire for a girl baby and a societal imperative to pretend an adopted child was just the same as a natural child. I was placed with my parents the way a piece of art is placed in a room—to complement the surrounding décor. My mother did not place me for adoption. She let Catholic Charities have me because she couldn't figure out a way, at sixteen years old, without a high school diploma, a job, or supportive parents, to keep me herself. There was no place for me in her home, no place for me in her family, no place else for me to go. For three months I stayed in a place where babies waited, separated from their mothers, to be adopted. Three months in a place without family of any kind, cared for by whom? Nurses? Employees? What kind of place was it? What color were the walls? How hot was it that summer? How did the sheets and blankets feel? In that place, what did they call me? My name was Kimberly. My mother wouldn't tell me why, a silence I was used to. In the place I grew up, there were many silences. I knew my place, needed always to remember my place. We visited the Lord's place every week. We never talked about displacement, mine, or replacement of my family with theirs, which I had to call mine. Replacement of my name. The affection I was to displace from one mother onto another. I was in the place of the child she could never bear, the child my father forsook by marrying her. (I had been forsaken.) Where is my place? I have made a place for myself—my own home, my own family, the only place that feels like mine.

MATERNITY HOME

A woman or girl who becomes pregnant but is not married must seek residence in a group home for women and girls such as herself. Why does she need to do this, presuming she had a perfectly good home to live in prior to becoming pregnant? Consider that she may end up in a group home because, upon becoming pregnant, she is no longer welcome in her own home, though she may be invited back once her unfortunate situation is dealt with.

Brochures for the earliest Crittenton homes in the 1890s commanded "Go and Sin No More." Founder Charles Crittenton wanted to rescue fallen women through religious conversion.

The Salvation Army's first rescue home for unwed mothers opened in 1886 "for young women who desire and are earnestly seeking the salvation of their bodies and souls."

At St. Ann's Infant and Maternity Asylum in Cleveland, Catholic nuns prayed that "the fallen one like Magdalene may repent and return to grace."

What began as a mission to help poor women and girls raise their babies and become contributing members of society evolved with the advent of adoption as a solution to illegitimacy. Maternity homes began to appeal to paying, middle-class families wanting to cover up indiscretions.

In 1965, two years prior to my conception, there were two hundred maternity homes across the United States.

My mother was not permitted to stay at the nearby maternity home. Her parents couldn't afford to pay. Neither was she welcome in the home where she'd grown up, though that is where she stayed, having no other option. Two years after my birth, at the age of eighteen, she got married and moved out. Ten years later, she got divorced.

In 1980—eight years after women's birth control became widely available and seven years after *Roe v. Wade*—the number of maternity homes nationwide had fallen to 99.

By 1993, 215 maternity homes were documented, and the number continues to increase.

The new maternity homes are smaller. Women and girls often stay with their babies for up to one year after birth. The homes teach life skills and offer high school classes. Some, though, only accept women planning to relinquish, and operate on the premise that these women need intensive treatment and counseling. They preach in favor of sexual purity and against both abortion and single parenting, much like the original maternity homes of the late nineteenth century.

Consider the need these homes fill. Consider how the need might better be met.

BEST INTERESTS OF THE CHILD

The child was clothed and fed. She was kept warm in winter and cool in summer. She had water to drink when she was thirsty. She wore new shoes each year. She slept in her own bed, in her own bedroom. The child lived in a house with doors that locked and windows that opened, a roof that did not leak, fresh paint on the walls, where the floors were clean, and so was the toilet, the refrigerator, every upholstered thing. The child spoke early. She learned her ABCs and 123s. The child attended a private school. The child went to church. The child read books and sang songs. She played outside in summer. She learned how to swim. The child always smiled in photos. The child was frequently told to smile at home, was asked why she was so sullen. The child learned where to sit. The child learned what should not be said. She wrote a poem in a card that made her mommy mad on Mother's Day. The child was told she cried for two weeks after they brought her home. The child learned her name. The child had dolls she loved. The child watched the girls at school swing their long hair. The child obeyed the teachers' rules. She brought home excellent report cards. The child made a best friend her mother didn't like. The child went steady with a boy and stayed at his house as often as she could. The child wanted to be hugged. She wanted someone to say "I love you." The child wanted to be seen. She stayed in her room and closed the door. The child fell in love and wondered if her mother had done the same. The child learned about the sin that created her. The child wanted to be holy. The child had lived in a home with other children. The child never learned about being born. The child explained why she couldn't wouldn't marry her cousin her brother. The child said she'd never seen her mother. The child had skin that burned. The child was a ghost. The child was stubborn bull-headed mouthy. Why did she always argue? The child would not sell her candy. The child learned how to be alone. The child was the good one, the smart one, the one who listened. The child was the one who always criticized, who never agreed. The child was the one who left. The child was the last one picked. The child crossed her arms over her budding breasts, bent over to hide them. The child never earned As from her English teachers. The child was never a favorite. The child was afraid she'd get pregnant. She cried on the front steps. The child dressed as a gypsy. The child stopped cutting her hair. She taught herself to sing. The child wrote poems. The child did not speak in the car. The child slapped her mom. The child was a photo in her father's wallet. The child walked barefoot on the grass. The child watched kids playing through the window. She wanted to go back to school. She stopped trying to join. The child learned to be quiet.

NORMAL

There exists a code of what is acceptable to most people in a society. Normal behavior. A normal house, a normal lifestyle. Normal development. A normal upbringing. A normal appearance. A normal course of events.

Normal is about conformity. It's about being inoffensive, not rocking anyone's boat.

Those who exist outside the parameters of what's considered normal can have difficulty finding acceptance. Adolescents are hyperaware of trying always to pass as normal, because being considered normal makes it easier to belong.

I was never normal. My conception, my birth, my adoption, my home life were all in some way outside the realm of acceptable. I was hyperaware of not being normal.

As I grew older, I realized that most people are in some way not normal. Most people's lives break some of the rules that I had internalized as the guidebook for normalcy.

More important was the discovery that there are different definitions of normal for different groups of people. I was abnormal in my environment partially because I was in the wrong environment, one that didn't fit me. I didn't have to stay there. I could relocate. I could find people who were more like me.

It's also a kind of freedom to live outside of normal, because you can be anything at all. When you let go of the idea that there are rules that must be followed, the limits on your life fall away, and everything is possible.

ORPHAN

UNICEF uses the word "orphan" to mean any child who has lost at least one parent to death. In 2015, there were nearly 140 million of these children around the world, though only 15.1 million of them had lost both parents, and the vast majority of all those kids defined as orphans were being cared for by family members. Only 5 percent were aged five and under.

I learned via the paper report of my own beginning that my father was an actual orphan. I was alone in my husband's childhood bedroom, him downstairs tending to his dying father, when I opened the letter I anticipated would tell me about my mother and discovered that my father had lost his own mother and father before I was born.

I am not an orphan. I never was. Neither were most of the adoptees I've come to know.

Both of my parents were alive when I was adopted, but both of my father's parents had died before I was conceived. He lived in an orphanage, multiple orphanages, separated from most of his siblings. He was seventeen when I was conceived. What could he have done? He had needed someone to take care of him. He had no way to care for me or for my mother, even if he had been her boyfriend, which he wasn't, or had believed he was my father, which he didn't at the time.

What if his parents had still been alive when I was born? Or, what if he, who is as stubborn as I am, had believed at the time that

I was his? Of course, none of the what-ifs matter, and the first one is ridiculous; if his parents had still been alive, he wouldn't have been in the orphanage in my mother's neighborhood, so very likely I wouldn't exist and neither would my children.

They told my husband the child he adopted from Korea was an orphan, but who knows. Other Korean adoptees have discovered parents still alive, still loving them across long years and miles. They've been welcomed back into whole families marked forever by the hole of losing them. "Orphan" was a word used to mean "available for adoption," no matter how the availability came to pass. Often, a child's availability was described as abandonment, but even this is questionable. Some children were taken from mothers, placed in orphanages without maternal consent.

You don't know what you don't know. My stepson, whom I only knew as an adult, was four when he came to the United States to be adopted. I suspect now that he was a paper orphan, that the documents sent with him to America were falsified. I suspect that he remembered his family, and that the memory once vivid became a haunting as he grew farther away from where he'd come. Nothing I suspect matters any more—or maybe it does. It can't help him in any way is what I mean.

If I hadn't met my stepson, I might not be writing this book. Is there someone out there looking for him, wondering what happened, the way my mother wondered about me and I about her before we met? I wonder if we'll ever know.

He felt twice orphaned, I think, just as I felt orphaned while I was growing up despite having parents, just as I feel orphaned now by estrangement, parented by ghosts.

PUTATIVE FATHER

Putative: assumed to exist or to have existed; alleged to be such.

About half of US states have registries on which unmarried boys and men can document that they've had sex with a girl or woman and wish to retain parental rights if she bears their child. Some other states allow a boy or man to claim paternity by filing an affidavit or acknowledgment. If the girl or woman decides to relinquish said child for adoption, the boy or man will be notified, although this notification does not necessarily imply that he will be able to participate in any decision made about the child. Registering his claim does not imply that a boy or man will be able to parent or even visit his child.

Being a biological father does not necessarily make one a legal father in this country. A mother typically becomes the sole custodial parent upon a child's birth, unless she is married (whether or not her husband is the child's biological father) or a man is present directly following the birth and consents to his name being listed on the birth certificate (whether or not he is the child's biological father).

Because state laws regarding legal paternity vary widely, mothers who plan to relinquish their babies sometimes abscond with them to other states in order to avoid interference from fathers. Adoption agencies sometimes discourage too much communication between expecting mothers and the fathers of their promised-for-adoption babies, though you won't find acknowledgment of this practice on their websites or in their brochures.

Fathers are going to court to fight for the right to parent their own children and losing to strangers who want to adopt.

Meanwhile, adult adoptees are begging their mothers to tell them who their fathers are and being answered with silence or lies.

With one breath we berate fathers who don't step up to take responsibility for their children, and with the next breath we declare that fathers don't matter at all.

A father is more than a signature on a check. He is more than the sperm that breached an egg's wall. A father is not just one man; he is the link to generations of blood relatives. When you deny a child access to her father, you rob her of an entire family.

My father is half of me. He matters.

DNA

Half from him, half from her. Twenty-three chromosomes in one sperm. Another twenty-three in one egg. They meet and form a new cell with twenty-three chromosome pairs. The cell divides, divides, divides, copying those twenty-three pairs over and over and over.

I am a machine built from fifty trillion cells, each containing a unique circuitry of genes.

Him and her, each with their own set of twenty-three pairs, every chromosomal couple made of halves inherited from its parents, my grandparents.

The random person generator spun and spit out a combo that became me. Here I am, favoring the ice cream flavor of the father who did not raise me and the color scheme of an aunt I only met after my own children were born. Here is my grandmother's hairline. Here are my mother's childlike hands. I purchased photographs from art shows to hang on my walls, unaware that my father was working to perfect his own photography skills. I served as stylist for my childhood friends' hair, not knowing that my mother worked in a salon.

We are born with default settings factory installed, though our instruction manuals may require interpretation. Attempts to reprogram us may result in unexpected outcomes. Efforts to reinitialize us may prove unsuccessful.

The way I'm drawn to water. The way I walk through trees.

Our cells contain all the evidence needed to determine origin as well as potential destiny for those who know the key to their code.

REDACT

1   a : Cross over with heavy black line

      b : Smudge out

2   : Deliberately leave off

3   : Pretend it isn't there : Pretend it never was

4   a : Hide

      b : Cover up, as in a crime

      c : Protect a dirty little secret

5   : Legally discriminate

6   : Attempt anonymity without any guarantee (see "DNA")

7   : Protect oneself from one's own child/past/mistake

8   a : Create an imaginary narrative in which one was never pregnant, never gave birth, never surrendered a child

      b : Refuse to face reality

9   : Deny involvement : Deny culpability

10   a : Attempt to make permanent the black hole in another's
      biological history

      b : Control

11   a : Obfuscate

      b : Cry "fake news"

12   : Do as you were told

13   a : Reject in the most cowardly way possible

      b : Declare your unwillingness to connect without the
      nuisance of having to communicate directly with the off-
      spring you wish to make permanently disappear

      c : Act with concern only for oneself

14   a : Leave again

      b : Reinjure

15   : Confirm your original action, whether or not it was
      originally your choice

16   : Choose the closet : Close the door and lock it : Seal all the
      windows and draw the drapes tight : Turn off all the lights

ABORTION

Every person walking the earth at this moment exists because their mother gave birth to them after they survived multiple months in utero. Every person walking the earth today could have been aborted, but wasn't. There is nothing about my status as an adopted person that makes me more likely to have been aborted than any other person.

Could I have been aborted? Sure. And you could have been aborted, too.

If I'd never been born, I wouldn't know the difference, and neither would the rest of the world. Every star in the night sky is another sun, millions upon millions of suns, each one potentially circled by planets, some of them potentially teeming with living organisms similar to those on our own planet. And if one of those organisms light-years away dies before being born, the rest of the universe continues swirling.

Because I was born, I became fully human, with all the needs and desires and rights of every other born human. If I hadn't been born, I never would have experienced the pain of grief or loneliness or rejection. I was born, and then I was surrendered, and throughout my life I've been in pain.

I was born, and I chose and was able to bear children of my own who are fully human. I have a daughter, and, because I know firsthand what it means to conceive, give birth to, and raise a child, I want every option for family planning to be available to her, without any burden of shame.

If my daughter becomes pregnant before she marries, the first decision she'll need to make is whether or not to endure nine months of growing a child in her belly. She'll have to consider her health, her circumstances, and her own feelings about the ethics of abortion. She'll have to examine her feelings about becoming a mother.

If she decides to carry this fictional baby to term, the next decision she'll have to make will be whether or not to raise her child herself. She'll have to consider her financial resources, her support system, and her own insight about the impact of different caregivers on child development. She'll have to consider her feelings for her child and her feelings about being a mother in the long term.

Whatever the outcome might be, if my daughter is ever in this situation, she will have not one, but two decisions to make. Adoption is not the opposite of abortion. Adoption is a choice made for a child's upbringing after the decision to carry a baby to term has already been made.

I was not relinquished for adoption as an alternative to being aborted. I was relinquished as an alternative to being raised by my own mother.

When I hear people advocating for adoption as a means of deterring abortions, I want to ask, why don't you care about the life of that pregnant woman as much as you care about the fetus inside her belly? Why don't you care enough about the life of a fully formed human woman to offer her the support she needs to be able to raise her own child?

I have seen adoption called the Catholic way to make a baby disappear, and I believe in my mother's case, this was true. I was disappeared rather than killed, but a part of me, along with a part of my mother, died just the same.

AMBIGUOUS

Ambiguous is shady, origin unknown.

We talk about grieving when someone dies. No one was dead.
Everyone was just missing, unknown to me, and I to them.

I was unknown to practically everyone.

I would have said I was curious, I would have said I thought
about it, about her, about what I might have had. I would not
have said I was in mourning. Whom have I had the right to
mourn? Mourning is a thing done in public. Privately, I only
cried. I was only lonely. I only imagined what might have been.

Once I made a friend I thought of as my sister, but after that
went sour, I never made that kind of friend again. Once someone said they'd seen me in a place I hadn't been, and I thought
maybe I had a sister out there, nearby. Once my sister sent me
fruit arranged like flowers in a cup. The fruit I ate; the cup I
use for tea. Once I put a picture of myself and my sister in a
frame with the word "sisters" on it. Now the frame is empty.

I've never seen my mother's natural hair color. I've never worn
her clothes.

Now my grief is known, identified, named. It is a real thing. I
have been in mourning for the relationship we could have devel-
oped, if she was able to admit I am her daughter. I mourn my
missing mother; my unmothered self mourns. I cry for the girl I

was and the woman I'll never be. I cry during every movie scene between a mother and child. I grieve the life I never lived, the love I was never able to give to anyone. The death of the person I never was and never will be.

I can no longer allow myself to dream of the parallel universe in which I am whole. I am learning, finally, to accept the fragmented me who lives here in this life of mine. We are never the same after we lose someone important to us. I lost the best version of me, a me who was treasured, loved. She remains ambiguous at best. How long will I grieve? Will there ever be a time when I don't feel both here and there, and therefore nowhere?

PRIMAL WOUND

Primal: of primary importance; native; basic; of earthly, bodily origin; as in primate; of biology and instinct; of the animal in us all.

Wound: an opening; a hurt; a cut, slice; damage; pain; a gaping hole; pus, blood, bacteria, scab, stitches; a gash; injury; scrape; burn; tear; scar.

An infant cannot express complex emotions via language. An infant can only thrash and cry and whimper and scream. An infant can feel all the pain of needles, pinches, bumps, and bruises; of too-loud sound and too-bright light, a too-hot or too-cold room; of hunger and thirst; of fear; of neglect. When an infant's needs are not attended to, an infant cries, and when its cries are not responded to, an infant learns that the world is cruel and empty, unloving, inhospitable. An infant leaves the warm safety of the womb to enter into the harshness of a hospital room, the hands of strangers, a plastic bed, the companionship of beeps and hisses. An infant recognizes her mother's voice and smell. She knows who is her mother and who is not. A missing mother creates a hole in the psyche that can never be healed, only scarred over, stitched closed as best as possible.

Human babies are not like sea turtle babies, born alone at night on a beach, left to find water on their own, embedded with an ancient homing instinct rather than the need for a mother. Humans are genetically closest to chimpanzees. We care for our young, feed them from our own bodies, teach them how to survive in the world. A child left to raise herself will be handicapped for life.

The infant was kept in the nursery. The infant was kept in a facility for waiting children, adoptable children, i.e., an orphanage. The infant was taken home by a man and a woman. The infant cried for two weeks. There was no consoling her.

ORIGINAL BIRTH CERTIFICATE (OBC)

When I was born at Booth Memorial Hospital in Cleveland, Ohio, a doctor used forceps to pull me by the skull out of my mother's body. He accomplished his goal at 6:00 p.m. My mother was alone, unmarried. She was not the only one in the room, of course. Nurses were there. And the doctor. And the baby—me. I had a birth day, the day I left my mother's body, the day someone cut the umbilical cord that linked me to her. I have a belly button to prove that I was born, just as every other person was born. They measured me. They weighed me. They ran all those newborn tests on me. They washed me and wrapped me in a blanket. They filled out a form: what was my mother calling me? Kimberly Ann. They gave me her last name. They wrote her name beside "Mother." They wrote no name beside "Father." They copied down my mother's address (the place where I lived inside her). They checked the box "Female." Her prior pregnancies? Zero. I was the first. First child, first grandchild. This was the document that described my birth. I am the person whose birth is described. I was born. I was named Kimberly. I was Kimberly as I lay in the hospital nursery. I was Kimberly when they (who?) transported me from the hospital to the baby home (how?). I was Kimberly as I grew there, slept there, ate there, shit there, learned my first words, smiled for the first time. I was Kimberly those three months, while my mother tried to find a way to keep me, when she signed me away, while my yet-unknown parents negotiated with Catholic Charities. I was Kimberly when those parents picked me up and took me home. They started calling me Karen, but legally, to the state of Ohio, to the county of

Cuyahoga, I was Kimberly. Legally, I was Kimberly on my first Thanksgiving, on my first Christmas. Legally, I was Kimberly on my first birthday, and my birth certificate accurately described the beginning of my life outside my mother's body. My mother's name and address were on my birth certificate as I experienced my second summer. My birth certificate described me until I was seventeen months old, when I was officially, legally adopted and my name was legally changed and the record of Kimberly's birth was overwritten.

LOST

They say you cannot lose what you never had, what was never yours. I was yours and, yes, you lost me. You let me go or you let go of me. I got away from you. And you were mine, if only in body, if only in name, if only for an instant. You were/are lost to me. I became lost. I am beyond reach. Lost implies someone who wanders aimlessly, or someone searching for something they cannot find. Lost implies discontent. I was lost to adoption. I would say this is true, because adoption took from me the link to another human body, to a family of human bodies, to the earth itself. It took belonging from me. I lost because of adoption. Lost can mean came in last place, was the loser in a competition or contest or game. The game of life, say. I feel adoption as a loss rather than a gain, a layer of unnecessary confusion and chaos in my life. Lost daughter. I am lost in relation to people with whom I share DNA, and they are lost to me. Lost sister. Lost aunt. Does losing require memory? If so, consider the second loss of those relatives postreunion. A loss is a loss is a loss. Someone told me recently that, because her parents both died shortly after she was born, she didn't remember them, and, therefore, her adoption contained no loss. I can't think of another circumstance in which a person would deny that the exit of her parents from her life was a kind of loss. Is the state of being lost a fact or an opinion? If I tell you I'm not lost, does that make it so? What if I tell you I am? What does an outsider's perception have to do with the fact of my relationship with another person? What if I'm lost to myself? Obscured, no longer visible. Being lost is something to save someone from, or to not allow to happen in the first place. Don't get lost! Stay close so I don't lose you! Not all those who wander are lost, but some who wander are lost, too (raises hand). You can't make someone un-lost by telling them they aren't lost, even if that someone is yourself. A thing once lost can be found, recaptured, held safe so as never to be lost again.

SURRENDER

No one surrenders unless they are coerced. The act of surrendering requires another person requesting or demanding acquiescence. A girl surrenders to the boy pressuring her to go further, to allow him to do more. Parents surrender their authority to teachers, to pastors and priests, to family elders, to the expectations of society. We surrender our will to God's, to our government's. Surrender is required of enlisted soldiers. We can't have them all exerting their own free will, thinking their own thoughts. We surrender when the cost is too high, when the pain is too much to bear. When we're worn out, freezing cold, burning hot. When our feet won't carry us anymore. When our brains shut down and we can't think straight. When we can't see straight. We surrender when we've been broken, as horses do. To surrender a child breaks a woman, destroys a girl, surely as if you broke a thousand boards across her back. No one surrenders who has the will and the means to fight. The ease of the surrender depends on how effectively a person's defenses have been worn down. No one asks for surrender without an ulterior motive, without wanting something, without the intent to win. A thing surrendered is a thing lost: virginity, innocence, a child, a life. To surrender is to be in a position of weakness, of vulnerability, to be overtaken, dominated. To be surrendered is to be let go, given up, to be without control over yourself. To be a thing exchanged in a war game. To be a prize of sorts. To be a punishment for the one who is made to surrender, a reminder of her weakness, her humiliation, of the lowest point in her life. To be surrendered is to be dehumanized, commodified, to become not even a victim, but only an object.

RELINQUISH

To relinquish implies a choice made willingly. It implies that what is given has value and that maybe there is some regret, or at least nostalgia, involved. If I relinquish my seat, that seat must have had some value or meaning for me, and I would have liked to have kept it. Relinquish doesn't imply force, so maybe agencies and adoptive parents like this word better. Maybe it alleviates some of their guilt. To be relinquished is to be important but not important enough, not something fought for but rather something offered up, like a sacrifice. Take this child and in exchange—what? Salvation? Perhaps something is promised in return, a payment of sorts, or a reward. Still, a trade takes place, and I am the thing traded, not quite a full human being, more an idea of a human being, the potential of one. I am a chip on the gambling table. I am the object described in the classified ad. I am the answer to someone's prayer, the bane of someone else's life. I exist only in relation to the parties involved in the trade. Relinquished—like an old car, like a favorite dress that no longer fits, like a rug that turned out to be not quite the right color—useful to someone, perhaps, but not to the original owner. Or like an apartment that's become unaffordable, despite how much it feels like home. Let go. Sent off. Like a dream with no chance of coming true. Like the last chance that didn't work out. Gone, not forgotten. Always remembered. Thought of fondly. Recollected. A whisper on the wind. An old song. A flashback. Relinquishing my dream of rejoining my family is what I'm left needing to do, because there's no other choice, not enough hope left to invest any more energy. I would like for adoption to relinquish me.

TERMINATION OF PARENTAL RIGHTS

You have the right to remain silent. Anything you say can and will be used against you, if not now, then later, someday, every day. Your silence is your best defense. Your silence is requested, expected, demanded. Look, right here it says you shall never speak of this again. It shall be as if it never happened. When they ask how many pregnancies you've had, calculate $x-1$, where x is the number of pregnancies you know you've had, and 1 is the pregnancy you'll never tell anyone about. Not your doctor, not your husband, not your (other) children. This is how you'll terminate your pregnancy without ever having an abortion. This is how you'll create a new life, how you'll split your life in two—before and after—how you'll split apart at your seams. You have signed away your rights: to your child, to identifying as a parent, to speaking of this at all. Look, it says right here you shall not ever try to find her, the baby. Not your baby anymore, you understand. You've been terminated, as her parent. A termination is permanent, like a death. It is a death of your right to behave as if you are somebody's mother. Not anymore you're not. The proof is right there, where you signed your name. That is your signature, isn't it? All loopy, like a little girl's signature. You were sixteen. And over the course of the next forty-nine years, you hardly ever mentioned it to anyone. Most people in your life don't even know you ever had another kid. The ones that do know don't ever bring it up. That's exactly how it was meant to be, exactly how they wanted it, how they wanted you—silent all these years. Complicit in the termination of your own right to act as a mother would act. You have not behaved as a parent despite being someone's mother. You behave like the girl who signed her name in loops and swirls. You behave like your girlhood was terminated too soon. You behave like someone who doesn't want to parent, who has accepted her own termination, who defends it now.

ADOPTABLE

Veronica became adoptable when her mother made an out-of-state adoption plan without informing her father. Her father fought in court in two states for four years to be allowed to raise his daughter, but ultimately lost her to the adoptive parents, who are unrelated to her biologically.

Noel became adoptable because his mother was underage, unmarried, disabled, and poor. His mother had been sexually abused for three years. His grandmother and a Department of Social Services caseworker decided he would be given up for adoption. His mother's wishes were not considered.

Hope became adoptable because her mother was homeless and drug addicted. The police officer who encountered her pregnant mother on the street offered to raise Hope. Her mother was not offered a home.

Myung-Sook became adoptable after getting lost in Seoul at eight years old. She told police officers how to find her father and elder siblings. They took her to a center for lost children. She told authorities there how to find her father and elder siblings. A man came and took her to an orphanage. She told the authorities at the orphanage how to find her father and elder siblings. They offered her for adoption, and she spent the rest of her childhood with strangers in America.

J became adoptable a second time when his first adoptive mother decided he was too much for her to handle. She hung a picture of his prospective new parents on the refrigerator.

In order for a child to become adoptable, something tragic must have happened. A mother deciding she is unwilling or unable to care for her own child. A mother being forced or coerced to give up her child to "better" parents. A child being kidnapped. Parents being too poor to provide for their child. Parents neglecting or abusing their child. Parents dying or being killed. Parents being separated from their child due to natural disaster, due to war, due to fear of punishment by their government, their society, their family.

I became adoptable because my parents were underage, unmarried, poor; because my father was an orphan; because my mother's father was domineering and unsupportive; because my mother's mother did not have the resources to support her; because my mother's church preached adoption as salvation for a girl who had disgraced herself; because there were married, childless couples seeking babies to raise as their own.

It is no gift to be adoptable. Would you who are raising a child now give your child as such a gift?

KIN

I used to make lists of all my relatives—my grandparents, my aunts and uncles, my cousins. I would count them and sort them, arrange them by age, group them by father's side vs. mother's side. I would examine the names, recite them. My brother and I were at the bottom of the list, youngest of the youngest. The list was mine but not mine. I claimed it as mine once upon a time, and then I began to stop making the list, to stop saying "my" when I talked about relatives. I began thinking in terms of Mom's sister, Dad's nephew. There was always an invisible membrane between me and them. I could observe them, I could offer their names to those who asked about kin, but I could not ever puncture the membrane to get to exactly where they were, the place where my mom's blood or my dad's blood pooled and flowed in rivers inside bodies that weren't their own. I could never compare my hair or eyes or skin to theirs and find someone like me. I could not speak their language, and they could not understand mine. They were mine only because they were the closest thing to kin that I had. Out in the world somewhere else were other people on my side of the membrane, people with my blood flowing through their bodies, people who spoke the language I knew. They were reading poems and singing songs and thinking about the leaves sprouting on trees in spring. They were redheaded and freckled, with eyes that color-shifted, as the sea does, depending on the light. I could not list their names. I could not recognize them on the street. But I could feel them, in the marrow of my bones. I could smell them on a summer day. When a patron came into the library where I worked and said he'd seen me riding my bike the other day on a street where I'd never ridden,

I knew they were close, that they would always be with me, that they always were. My kin came through Pennsylvania, through New York, from across the Atlantic, from islands, from centuries-old towns. I came alive on their river of blood.

HOME

Home base: a place where you're safe.

Home front: a line you'll defend.

Homebody: one who prefers home to anyplace else. Isn't that all of us? What is home if not the place we prefer?

Is home a place or a feeling?

The total ease I experience alone with my husband and kids, when I'm not actually alone at all. The freedom to be alone when I need to be without being forgotten or left behind.

Total engagement. Flow. The sense of needing nothing I don't have in this moment.

The sea. The sensation of a place or a person being exactly right without any cognitive understanding of why.

The ability to recognize home becomes distorted after you are uprooted from where you naturally fit. You learn to distrust your instincts. The ability to create an appropriate place for yourself becomes impaired.

No one can teach a person what home should be, because home is different for each of us. It's a particular comfort that depends on an individual's experience and personality.

Home is a longing for the perfect fit, for a place that feels balanced, comfortable, and secure. Home is a launch pad, providing all the fuel you need to go and explore, and it is a retreat, welcoming you back upon your return.

Love in the shape of walls and windows, gardens and waterways, arms and words.

GEOMETRY

Triad: birth parents, adoptive parents, adoptees. Alternative: triangle, as in love triangle, as in one child caught between two families, the child an unwilling participant in the tryst with all its secrets and lies. As in trinity, as if we are all one.

Circle: all parties equally spaced along a curved wheel, but who is driving? Certainly not the adoptee, who may feel, rather, that she is being circled by sharks. Best not to splash much or to wear bright colors. Best to blend in.

What is the shape of chaos, of a tangle? A thorny bramble?

Some picture a tree with its branches and roots, a place for everyone.

How about a cloud, sometimes pleasant, other times foreboding, either cirrus or a heavy, shapeshifting blanket. Call it a happy, fluffy cloud in a sunny blue sky if that fits. Or call it a tornado-spawning supercell. It's all a matter of perspective, of your position as meteorologist or storm chaser or pine tree or old barn roof.

A many-faced polyhedron. Which side is dominant? Where is the power angle? And why is it spinning? How do I get off?

REUNION

No one expects when they go to a reunion that they will, afterwards, keep in touch forever, pick up right where they left off, resume a full relationship. Think about high school reunions, reunions with former coworkers. Even family reunions. Distant relatives get together every few years for a day or a weekend, and then, afterwards, they go back to their own, individual lives.

This is how I got my heart broken: I imagined you, every day. I thought I knew that you loved me, that you had wanted to keep me. I thought I knew something no one ever told me. And maybe I wasn't wrong about that. But I expected us to pick up where we left off, as mother and daughter combined. I expected to return to you as your family. But you had gone on without me. And, to be honest with myself, I had gone on, too.

Some people better prepare themselves for possible outcomes, so they don't end up so brokenhearted when it doesn't work out. Sometimes it does work out, because both parties want the same level of relationship.

I don't regret finding you. I regret not thinking it through. We reunited as virtual strangers, though we felt we knew each other, too. Adoptees can anticipate possible outcomes, but no one can really prepare for how it feels to instinctively know your mother and yet not know her at the same time. No one can prepare for the shock of losing her a second time, the pain that shoots through your body, the way you'll crumple to the ground, retreat to your bed to escape into sleep.

I don't regret trying.

BIRTH FAMILY

I am a mother because I gave birth to my children. I am their birth mother. Most mothers in the world are birth mothers. Giving birth is the natural course of events, the way humans and other animals perpetuate our species and avoid extinction.

I call my mother my birth mother when I need to distinguish her from my adoptive mother in a conversation. Otherwise, I call her my mother, or I use her name. When I address her directly, I call her Mom. I know to whom I'm speaking. When I think of her, I think, My mother. I think, This woman gave birth to me. I think, I lived inside her body once, I carry her genes. I think, I wish we could be together.

We don't say a child has a stepmother and a birth mother; we say stepmother and mother, because divorce doesn't change the fact of who gave birth to a child. It would make sense also to say a child has an adoptive mother and a mother, though some would find this offensive, claiming the term mother should be reserved for the primary caretaker. If so, shouldn't a child primarily living with her father refer to his new wife as mother and use birth mother to refer to the woman who bore her?

When I think of my father, he is just my father, the man who impregnated my mother when he was still a boy, the man who has told me he will never deny me. I call him birth father when I need to clarify which father I'm speaking about. Otherwise, I call him Dad.

I am a daughter to four people. I am an adopted daughter to two people. I am a birth daughter, a birth child, to two people. I was born, just like everyone else. Everyone is a birth child. You, reading this, you're a birth child.

Birth is a term that signifies the experience of being born, or of being related to someone because of common blood, common genes. The term is only derogatory when one uses it to minimize the importance of biology in human connectedness. For example, when a pregnant woman is referred to as a birth mother prior to actually giving birth, prior to seeing or holding her own child, prior to her child being placed for adoption, prior to there being any need to distinguish her from any other mother, because she is the only mother.

The natural mother is the birth mother, because birth is an occurrence of nature taking its course.

FIRST

You want me to call you my first, but you are not the first one I remember. I was too young, too unformed. My brain wasn't yet primed. The first one I remember is the one who was with me when I became aware, consciously, of myself as a being separate and distinct from any other being. Before that moment, I just was, and I was a part of you. We were one being, and then we weren't. And it happened too quickly, too soon. I adapted. I had to. I'm a survivor, like you. Technically, sure, you were the first, but that's not how I think of you, or her. I don't rank you. First can also mean best, like first prize or first place or first in my heart. I was your firstborn child, but I'm certainly not first in your life. This isn't a competition. The first memory I have of seeing you was in a photo on my computer screen. No one can be first in my life anymore besides me. Some say first is the worst. Some thirst to be first. I never use this term, not ever. It's unscientific. It's inaccurate. It's imprecise. I am a daughter and you are a mother. Isn't that enough? You missed my first step, first word, first tooth, first haircut, first crush, first time. First heartbreak, though, you were there for that. And first love. First heartbeat. First movement. You fed me my first meal, provided my first shelter. That day I brought you flowers was not the first time we met.

UNPLANNED/UNEXPECTED CHILD

To plan for a child is to intentionally try to become pregnant, to attempt to conceive a child. The best plans are subject to destruction. An unexpected pregnancy can happen to just about anyone who has sex. The stigma surrounding unplanned pregnancies and unplanned children has to do with the idea that a woman or girl should not be having sex if she doesn't want to become pregnant. We enforce this by shaming women and girls who do have sex outside of marriage. We don't tend to shame boys in the same way, to the same extent, because boys and their families don't have to deal with many of the consequences of becoming pregnant. Boys have more freedom to walk away from a pregnancy, to wash their hands of it, to leave it up to the girl. A man doesn't have to consider health risks to his own body during nine months of growing another human being or during the event of that human being exiting his body somehow, some way. Men and boys want to have sex with us, pressure us for sex, without worrying too much about pregnancy, often without even asking about birth control. It costs many thousands of dollars to endure a pregnancy, to give birth, to care for a child until they are grown and can care for themselves. In 2017, the estimated cost of raising a child from birth to age seventeen for a lower-income family was close to $175,000. That's more than $10,000 per year. And that's after shelling out anywhere from $5,000 to over $10,000, depending on the state you live in, for an uncomplicated vaginal delivery. An unexpected pregnancy is no joke. But it happens, and it's not a thing to be ashamed of unless you've been shamed about sex itself. Unplanned does not equal unloved, yet an unplanned child is a big deal, from every standpoint: emotional, physical, financial. An unplanned child is only a crisis, though, when a pregnant woman or girl lacks the support she needs, when she has no one to lean on for help. Taking her child from her is not support. I was unplanned and unexpected, but I was not unwanted or unloved. It can feel as if I was discarded. As if my mother was discarded because she had sex and became unexpectedly pregnant. My own children were unplanned and unexpected at the times they were conceived. The difference between me and my mother was that I was older, I was financially secure, and I had a supportive partner. These things matter. I often wonder how our lives would have been different, hers and mine, if someone had helped her keep me.

BABY SCOOP ERA

I am one of roughly two million people who were surrendered for adoption as babies in the United States during the 1960s. Prior to 1973, more than 19 percent of children born to white, unmarried mothers were relinquished for adoption.

My mother is one of around four million mothers who lost children to adoption during the Baby Scoop years, between 1940 and 1970.

Why?

Joseph H. Reid, executive director of the Child Welfare League of America, declared his opinion in 1956: "The concept that the unmarried mother and her child constitute a family is to me unsupportable."

In the 1950s, women who engaged in sex without marriage were deemed to have personality disorders. In 1965, Sr. Joseph Marie, director of social services at the DePaul Infant and Maternity Home in Cleveland—where I resided in the months prior to my adoption—described her institution's purpose: "since science is beginning to understand more clearly the psychological patterns which often lead to pregnancy out-of-wedlock, the entire living experience at DePaul is focused on treatment."

When did you first have sex? When did you first want to kiss someone romantically?

I was fourteen when I was first kissed, and I wanted that kiss. There was nothing wrong with me.

> Most of the girls labored alone. The majority knew little about what to expect physically or emotionally from childbirth. . . . Unlike the grief over the death of a child, which is permanent and for which there is an established grieving process, the loss of a child through adoption has no clear end and no social affirmation that grief is even an appropriate response. (Ann Fessler, *The Girls Who Went Away: The Hidden History of Women Who Surrendered Children for Adoption in the Decades Before Roe v. Wade*)

For every baby available for adoption, there were ten couples waiting to adopt. Demand exceeded supply. Adoption was sold to childless couples on the premise that relinquishing mothers simply did not want their babies.

My mother says she did not want to give me up. The social workers she interacted with during her pregnancy and after my birth repeatedly pressured her to sign my surrender. They told her I would be better off. They told her that her parents shouldn't be made to pay for her mistakes. She was sixteen. She tried to hide from them in the bathroom of her hospital room. She went home without signing the paper. She cried every night. She managed to hold them off for five and a half weeks. When she ran out of ways to hide, she was forced to sign.

"A sexually active teen who does not use contraceptives has a 90% chance of becoming pregnant within a year," according to the Guttmacher Institute.

The birth control pill, though approved by the FDA in 1960, was not widely available to single women until 1972. Abortion became legal nationwide in 1973.

On average, people in the United States have sex for the first time at age seventeen. The vast majority of teens having sex these days are using contraceptives, and condoms are their preferred choice. In 2013, less than 5 percent of girls aged fifteen to nineteen became pregnant, a record low.

In 2012, under 120,000 children were adopted in the United States. This figure includes all ages and races of children, which implies that white infant adoptions have declined exponentially compared to the 1960s.

In 2017, $200 million was redirected away from teen pregnancy prevention programs. Grants originally intended to last five years were cut off after only three years. Conservatives in the federal government began reshaping these programs to push abstinence-only initiatives rebranded as "sexual risk avoidance." Conservatives also want to dismantle health insurance coverage for contraceptives guaranteed by the Affordable Care Act and restrict access to family planning providers.

The Catholic Church continues to forbid contraception, even for married couples.

ANGER

Say I'm angry. It's all right. Anger is an appropriate response to injustice.

Anger develops when one experiences pain that has been inflicted by another, intentionally or not.

There's a lot for adopted people to be angry about. Losing our biological families. Losing our genetic and cultural heritage. Losing our sense of self. All because of choices made by others on our behalf when we were too young and helpless to have any control over those decisions.

Adoption doesn't happen organically. Adults make choices that result in children being shuffled from one family to another. It should come as no surprise that some of those children aren't very happy with the choices that were made.

On top of the losses inherent in every adoption, a significant number of adopted children end up with less-than-stellar adoptive parents, because adoptive parents are no different than natural parents in their human failings. Adoptive parents fight and drink, and abuse drugs, and abuse or neglect each other, and abuse or neglect their children, just as biological parents do. It should come as no surprise that children who 1) have experienced the losses previously described here and 2) are raised by less-than-stellar adoptive parents feel a good deal of anger about their situations.

Anger can be a mask hiding deeper, painful feelings: powerlessness, self-loathing, shame.

Anger can be a form of self-soothing, or self-medication, if you will. Focusing on the culpability of others takes the pressure off oneself.

Often, I become inexplicably angry over slights that, to others, seem small and insignificant. This is anger protecting me before I get cut, the voice of the child inside me who wants to feel safe.

Once, in my early twenties, I got out of my car in the middle of the street to argue with another driver, over what I can't recall. What was I so mad about that I stopped traffic to argue with a stranger? My anger was persistent, always near the surface, ready to rage. I was on high alert for potential threats from any direction. I think of this now as fuzzy anger, and I recognize that it is not productive or healthy, though it's a hard habit to break.

It's important to learn how to settle oneself, how to calm down and think through a situation rationally, to avoid responding in anger. It's important to remind myself that I am in control of my life now, that I am just as valuable as anyone else. It's important to remind myself that I don't need to allow anyone to repeatedly hurt me, and that I can keep myself safe through means other than anger or aggression. I can describe how I feel and how I want to be treated. I can ask for what I need and refuse what causes me pain or stress. I can decide who to allow into my life and who to keep at a distance.

And I can use my anger productively, to challenge injustice, to keep me pumped for the fight.

ACTIVIST

Capital A. Small a. For many, there are enough a's already: adoptable, adoption, adopted, adoptee.

None of us is required to do anything at all.

Perhaps it's enough to get through this life. This day. Enough to find someone to love and to continue loving them. Enough to experience joy.

Perhaps it's enough to know your own parents. To meet them once. Or one of them. To talk on the phone. To exchange a text. To see a picture. To read a name.

Perhaps learning your own history is enough. Learning the world's history as it pertains to your own history.

For some, it's not enough. Some need to do something about it all. Big something, small something, anything at all, as long it's something, and it helps in some way.

We are all activists, perhaps. No capes, yet we are heroes of our own lives. Heroes on an as-needed basis, and that is enough. Sometimes it has to be.

I am putting these words down on paper. For now, for me, that is enough.

ILLEGITIMATE

On my legitimate (true)/illegitimate (not legal) birth certificate, there is a box labelled "LEGITIMATE (Specify yes or no)" containing a typed word, "NO." On my illegitimate (false)/ legitimate (legal) birth certificate, this box is deliberately left off. I was legitimately (according to accepted standards) illegitimate (born to an unmarried woman), but through adoption I was remade into a legitimate (made through legal procedure equal in status to one so conceived or born) child. I am a legitimate (conforming to recognized principles of hereditary right) heir to my adoptive parents' estate. Certainly, I am a legitimate (real) person. I am not a fairy or a figment of anyone's imagination. Though, if I'd never been adopted, my original birth certificate marking me as illegitimate (bastard) would have remained legitimate (allowed according to law) throughout my life. Presumably there are people who have gone through their whole lives presenting their legitimate (official) birth certificates marking them as illegitimate (misbegotten) to authorities. Would the blank line where my father's name should be not have been enough? Before I ever saw this blank space, solely on the basis of the story I was told about my birth, I recognized myself as a wayward child. No one had to tell me about the "NO" on my illegitimate (departed from the regular) birth certificate. So much rests on a father, no matter who the mother, no matter the child.

ADOPTEE

I am an adoptee. Legally and socially, adoption is what links me to one family, the family in which I was raised, and what separates me from the families of my biological mother and father. I am different in this way from other children, other daughters. My difference is not something to be either ashamed or proud of. It simply is. Adoptee is my reality.

There is not any moment when I'm not an adoptee. When I buy groceries, I'm an adoptee, though it doesn't matter very much then. When I go to the doctor, it matters quite a lot that I'm an adoptee. I'm an adoptee when I attend a PTA meeting or sit in a church or brush my hair. Every time I look in the mirror, I see an adoptee.

I hug my children as an adoptee. I kiss my husband as an adoptee.

Once upon a time, a long time ago, for an instant, I was not an adoptee. I was a fetus growing inside my mother's belly, then I was an infant descending through my mother's birth canal, exiting her body through her vagina, and I was her natural daughter. But when I was given to a new mother and father, and papers were signed, and a judge made me theirs, I became an adoptee.

I cannot choose not to be an adoptee. There is no end to it, just as there's no end to being someone's child. There's no reversing childhood. There's no erasing those formative years spent away from my biological kin. There's no way to become who I would have been if I hadn't been adopted. Reunion can't do it. Therapy can't do it. I can only live the best life I can, right now, as an adult adoptee.

MIRROR

Today my daughter wore a shirt of mine to school, and it fit her body the way it used to fit mine. She can just about wear my shoes.

My son looks like I did in pictures when my hair was cut short. He has my wave in his hair, too, and my freckles. He has my father's forehead.

When I looked in the mirror as a child, I saw a big nose, a huge forehead, brows with no arch, skin too ghostly white, teeth too dominant, eyes that squinted shut when I smiled. As a teen, I saw thighs that were too fat, a stomach not flat enough. I saw hair that was too thin, too red, too straight, and always too short, because my mom didn't understand why anyone would want long hair.

I saw no one who looked like me. I was an odd creature, dropped from who knows where. I noticed all the large and small ways my friends resembled their parents and siblings and even cousins. I knew it must feel wonderful to look like someone else, because people talked about looking like such-and-such relative all the time.

When I was a young adult, I wouldn't leave the house without first putting on makeup and styling my hair. I avoided meeting anyone's eyes. If I didn't look at them, maybe they wouldn't see me. I was awful to see.

I see my kids now so comfortable in their own skin, so confident. Sure, they sometimes exhibit self-doubt, but I have never moved through the world with my head up the way they usually do. I can't stop looking at them. I study them. I watch their expressions, listen to how they speak, and wonder which ancestor they might be channeling.

After my daughter was born, I began seeing myself differently in pictures. It was the strangest sensation, as if I'd somehow transformed into a perfectly acceptable-looking human being without having changed anything at all about my outward appearance. I began seeing her in me. How could I have made such beautiful children if I was so ugly? Logic told me I must not be ugly after all.

Now that I've seen my parents and siblings and photos of my biological ancestors, I understand why I look the way I do. I understand that I look like other people in the world, many other people, and when I see my people, I see their beauty. But I still can't quite see myself clearly. I doubt I ever will.

WELFARE

How did you fare? Did you fare well? Was the journey smooth, untroubled?

We enter through a tunnel from water, from darkness. We come out into harsh light, many voices, cold. We are lifted, we are handled, we are wrapped.

Was I held? How was I fed? Was I rocked, was I sung to? Did anyone whisper my name in my ear? Did anyone inhale my smell?

The journey was rough and lonely. I kept looking for someone I recognized, but there was never anyone there. I was always looking, always seeking, always searching.

It probably seems as if I've fared pretty well. I made As in school. I found jobs. I fell in love. But why did I have to spend years of my life searching for what I originally had? Why did I have to lose it at all?

No one followed up on me. No one represented me. I was not a party to my own proceeding. They'll say it was all for the welfare of my mothers, but both of them are miserable now, as I have been. Fare thee well, do-gooders.

Am I well? I'm not sure. I am more well than I was. I hope I will be better yet.

SECRET

If you keep your child a secret, she will write this book.

If you keep your child's story secret, she will write this book.

If you keep secrets, your child will write this book.

If your secret is your child, she will write this book.

If your child is secret, she will write this book.

If your child won't keep secrets, she will write this book.

If your child writes this book, she is done with secrets.

AFFAIR

I have a secret—I always loved my mother. I loved her in private, in my heart, in my imagination, in fantasies I never told anyone about, an ongoing affair of my own making that went on all throughout my childhood. She was mine alone, a treasure I kept to myself. No one could take her from me.

My parents did not have an affair. An affair is not a one-time thing. They had no relationship at all. Before I learned this, I imagined them in love. Who doesn't wish themselves conceived from love? And lots of babies are conceived this way, but let's be real, lots of babies aren't. Many babies are accidents, whoopsies, too soon or too late, unintended. I'm not the only one, by a long shot.

I've been in what people would generally call an affair, what I call an affair. Anyone who's had an affair knows how guilt and shame feel, and that affairs are costly and painful. In an affair, you are not real in another person's life—you are an extra, on the side, disposable. You only become visible when the other person allows it. You are insignificant.

When your mother wants to have a relationship with you in secret, behind the backs of her other family members and her close friends, it's painful, and it's no less guilt ridden or shameful than the most difficult romantic affair. It is love on condition of one's total abandonment of self-regard. What would I do to have the love of the person I dreamed of my entire life? How much of myself would I give up in exchange? My mother will not fight for me or stand beside me. She is content to settle for the residue of what was one of the most important relationships of both of our lives.

I refuse.

GRIEF

Begin with the lifeless body on a hospital gurney, a tube still lodged in his mouth, the room full of people who told you what you already knew from the cop on the phone.

Trace it back to the anger, the multiple disappearances, the day spent trying to convince him not to use a knife on himself.

He said in Atlanta there were so many Koreans but nowhere he fit in, not knowing the language, not knowing the customs, having forgotten his own name, the names of his parents. But not having forgotten at all, ever, not even once, not even for a moment.

Grief lies dormant, or so we think, except that it doesn't, not really. Really, it's everywhere, all the time, making me yell and want to smash things. And sit for long hours in a dark room. And run away.

Grief is searching every face for your own, on the street, in the store, in a magazine, in a Sunday ad. Missing someone you can't remember, whom you wouldn't know if you sat beside them. Knowing they're nearby, feeling them.

Never being invited to Thanksgiving dinner. Not being welcome.

Wondering who you could've been. Not knowing who you are right now.

A baby crying for two weeks, inconsolable, after more than three months away from her mother. How many days of those months were also spent crying?

Grief begins with strange smells, strange hands, strange voices. Being wrapped in strange blankets, dressed in strange clothes. Everyone talking in a language you don't understand, being unable to make yourself understood. You can't describe how it is to feel you could be disappeared at any time. Nothing is permanent. No one stays. No one keeps you for very long. You keep your head down, try to do what they want, try to be someone they want.

The fear that every airplane carrying your husband on a business trip will fall from the sky. The fear that your son won't come home from a friend's house, that the siren you hear is an ambulance rushing to the crash site where your daughter's bus has overturned.

Weeping through every movie, song, book, TV commercial. Tears every time you speak of it. Wondering how much crying a body can withstand in a lifetime. Being unable to cry when your mother holds you in her arms.

The loss of ancestry, of connectedness to humanity, to another human body, to a lineage of human bodies. The inability to give your children an extended family of related people who treasure them, who want to know them and be involved in their lives.

All the mistakes you make trying to give them what you lost.

ADVERSE CHILDHOOD EXPERIENCES (ACEs)

There is a strong link between childhood trauma and social, emotional, and chronic medical issues in adulthood.

Heart disease. Lung cancer. Diabetes. Autoimmune disorders.

Score one for each "yes" answer.

Did a parent often verbally assault you, insult you, humiliate you?

Did a parent cause you physical harm or attempt to?

Toxic stress physically damages a child's developing brain.

Did you feel no one loved you? Did you feel unimportant?

Was your family not what you would call close?

The higher your score, the higher your risk.

The tendency to inflict violence. The tendency to become a victim of violence.

Did your parent drink too much? Did your parent use?

Was your parent mentally ill? In prison? Abused by someone else?

Other types of trauma exist that are not on the list. Score these, too.

Accidents. Illnesses. Deaths.

Losing a caregiver.

With a score of four or more, likelihood of depression increases 460 percent. Likelihood of suicide increases 1,220 percent.

ATTACHMENT

In the late 1960s, John Bowlby concluded that childhood development depends heavily on a child's ability to form a strong relationship with at least one primary caregiver. This relationship provides a necessary sense of security for the child, a strong foundation, and those without such an attachment are fearful throughout their lives. They are less willing to seek out and learn from new experiences. Disrupting an attachment relationship can have severe consequences that last a lifetime.

Later, Mary Ainsworth observed what she called "attachment behavior," wherein insecure children attempted to establish or reestablish an attachment to an absent caregiver. They would cry and demonstrate great distress until they were reunited with the caregiver.

Beginning in 1957, Harry Harlow studied social interaction by removing infant rhesus monkeys from their mothers and from other monkeys. Infant monkeys who were offered inanimate surrogate mothers preferred those they could snuggle against to those that only provided food. Monkeys kept in isolation for too long never learned to communicate or socialize with other monkeys.

Rarely, a child who has experienced extreme neglect during early childhood may be diagnosed with Reactive Attachment Disorder (RAD), the earliest definition of which appeared in the *Diagnostic and Statistical Manual of Mental Disorders* (DSM) in 1980. RAD does not appear in children who did not experience severe neglect, and the majority of neglected children are able to form attachments after being placed in more caring, supportive homes, although this takes some time, and the attachments formed may be less than perfect. Symptoms of true RAD are observed by the time a child is five years old. As a child ages, other developmental factors come into play that fog the view of what is actually going on.

The quality of a child's caregiver matters. Children with RAD will be further traumatized by new parents who are overly authoritarian or who have negative perceptions of their children. True emotional attachment is neither equivalent to nor evidenced by obedience.

In 1987, Cindy Hazan and Philip Shaver concluded that the way adults in romantic relationships form attachments with each other is similar to the way parent/child attachments are formed. Adult relationships function best when both parties are able to balance intimacy with independence.

Later research found that both infants and adults attach to others on a spectrum based on degrees of anxiety and avoidance in their relationships. While early-childhood attachments undoubtedly influence adult relationships, a person's attachment style can change over time with exposure to new social experiences.

ADOPTION

The act of permanently, legally transferring responsibility for a child from one caregiver to another. Often includes a tax credit and days off from work for the adoptive parents.

The experience of being permanently, legally transferred from one caregiver to another, for a price. Frequently, the new caregiver is a stranger and the new home is unfamiliar. Frequently, contact with the original/previous caregiver (including but not limited to photos, phone calls, knowledge of names and locations, etc.) is thereafter prohibited.

When a child is adopted from foster care, the cost of the adoption typically is covered by the state, and adoptive parents usually receive financial assistance for the ongoing care of the child. When a child is adopted via other means, whether domestically or internationally, adoptive parents pay as much as $50,000 in expenses and fees. Because African American children are less desired by prospective adoptive parents, their adoption fees are often lower.

Puppies are typically offered for adoption when they are about eight weeks old, having had sufficient time to wean from their mothers yet being still young enough to train so as to fit with their new owners' lifestyle and preferences. Human children may be transferred to their new caregiver immediately following birth or at any point between birth and adulthood. In 2007, about eighteen thousand US newborns were placed with nonrelative adoptive parents. Older children are less likely to be adopted from foster care than younger children. In all cases, the new caregiver is permitted to rename the adoptee. In all cases, the adoptee is expected to bond with the new caregiver and is considered deviant if this bonding, known as attachment, does not take place or if the development of true, loyal feelings for the new caregiver takes longer than expected or desired.

PARENT

Few people are prepared to become parents. The best preparation often becomes useless when reality differs from what was expected or planned for.

When I was a young girl, I dreamed of having a big family, five or six kids. I planned to start early. I didn't want to be an old mother like my mom was. I'm sure when she was a young girl, my mom also imagined the children she would have. Her sister and brother got started before she did. She was the unfortunate one. Her body failed her. She became my mom through adopting me. I don't imagine that was her dream.

The mother who gave birth to me barely had time to dream at all of how she would one day become a parent. One day she was a regular high school girl, one day she noticed a cute boy, one day she ended up alone with him, one day she realized she was pregnant, one day her mother found out, one day she met a social worker, one day she gave birth, one day she went home without a baby, one day she signed a paper, one day.

I didn't get pregnant by my first boyfriend, or my second. I didn't get pregnant young, as I'd wanted. I didn't get married first, didn't make any kind of good plan. I became pregnant, unexpectedly, at age thirty-two. I was both prepared and unprepared to become a mother—prepared, because I'd wanted it for so long, and spectacularly unprepared, because my partner and I were still working out our relationship, because I didn't know how I would cope financially, because it happened unexpectedly. I gave birth to a child who was unplanned, who made me and his dad into parents, the same way my birth made my mother and father parents, the way my adoption made my mom and dad parents.

Truly, my mom and dad were the most prepared of us all, having had to initiate the adoption, adoption not being something that can just happen unexpectedly. But I was not and am not any less of a parent for having been less prepared.

I have four parents rather than the traditional two. Some kids have only one. My father had none at the time I was born, both of his having died. Today I have three alive. My husband has none left.

Is a parent still a parent after death? Of course. Then a parent must also remain a parent after surrender, after relinquishment, after estrangement.

CHOICE

My mother was fifteen when I was conceived, sixteen when I was born. Her father was so ashamed, he made her hide when relatives came to their house. He wouldn't allow an aunt on her mother's side of the family to raise me. He preferred me to disappear, in the Catholic way.

When I turned sixteen, I had a shelf of stuffed animals in my bedroom. I drew hearts around my boyfriend's name in the margins of my notebook. I hadn't yet earned my driver's license or started working at my first job. If I had become pregnant, I would not have been able to feed, clothe, or provide medical care for my child without my parents' help. I would have had to live with my child in their home. I probably would not have graduated high school on time or gone to college right away.

Although I'd had a steady boyfriend for two years by that time, at sixteen I had never had a conversation with my parents about birth control. I was still seeing a pediatrician for medical care. And my boyfriend was too embarrassed to buy condoms himself. What if someone recognized him? We were taught that the rhythm method was the only birth control allowed for Catholic married couples. Unmarried people like us were supposed to remain abstinent.

In 1967, when my mother became pregnant with me, the age of majority in Ohio was twenty-one, which meant her parents would have needed to consent in order for her to be prescribed birth control. The right of married couples to use contraception had been granted by the Supreme Court only two years prior, and many states would deny birth control to unmarried women until another Supreme Court ruling in 1972. Abortion would not be legalized in most states until 1973.

Maternity homes for unwed mothers were booming in the 1960s, but my mother didn't stay in one, because her parents couldn't afford it. Instead she endured being hidden away in plain sight like a shameful story. She endured her father's rage. The Catholics had little charity for her. They wanted to be paid. After counseling and labor and delivery, she owed them. I was her price.

Don't tell me my mother made a choice, as if her life as a sixteen-year-old girl in 1968 was her own. Don't tell me any girl has a choice that is not permitted to her by her parents or her culture. Don't tell me any woman has a choice that is not permitted to her by her circumstances.

Don't tell me I was chosen. My mom couldn't become pregnant because she'd had a hysterectomy, so she and my dad decided to adopt a baby. A baby, any baby. I was offered to them, assigned to them because I was similar enough in skin tone and ancestry to be able to pass as theirs. They didn't choose me. They chose to adopt. I was the child they got, like it or not.

My mother didn't choose, my parents didn't choose, and I certainly didn't choose.

I became a product to be sold. I was interchangeable with any number of other babies whose mothers likely also had no real choice about surrendering them. I had no choice about where or with whom I grew up. I did not choose to have my name changed or my birth certificate falsified.

I have a choice now. I choose how much or how little of what I was born with or what I absorbed during my childhood to incorporate into my adult life. I choose to be open and honest with my own children about their family and its secrets, its problems, its shame. I choose to face my grief, to process it, to learn how to live with so much incredible loss. I choose to love despite so much fear, despite repeated rejection, despite constant pain.

I choose to love. I choose to enjoy my life. I choose to own my life.

I choose to speak. I choose the name I use. I choose to claim even those ancestors who chose not to claim me.

I choose to fight for the rights of mothers and fathers to raise their own children, for children to know their mothers and fathers.

I choose truth.

SOURCES AND SUGGESTED READING

The lexicon presented here is created in part as a response to the list of terms described as Positive Adoption Language by Marietta Spencer in her article "The Terminology of Adoption" published in *Child Welfare* in 1979 and as Respectful Adoption Language by Patricia Irwin Johnston in her 2004 essay "Speaking Positively: Using Respectful Adoption Language." Johnston's essay can be accessed at a number of locations on the Web, including http://www.barkeradoptionfoundation.org /speaking-positively-using-respectful-adoption-language. As of this writing (March 30, 2018), the *Wikipedia* page on "Language of Adoption" seems to present a fairly accurate history of this type of terminology: https://en.wikipedia.org/wiki /Language_of_adoption.

Standard definitions, where given, are from *Merriam-Webster* online: www.merriam-webster.com. *Merriam-Webster* does not list the term "birthmother" as all one word. Rather, the phrase "birth mother" is listed—the noun "mother" modified by another noun, "birth," similar to the phrase "adoptive mother," both phrases signifying "mother."

These books are referenced in numerous entries:

Fessler, Ann. *The Girls Who Went Away: The Hidden History of Women Who Surrendered Children for Adoption in the Decades Before Roe v. Wade.* New York: Penguin Press, 2006.

Morton, Marian J. *And Sin No More: Social Policy and Unwed Mothers in Cleveland 1855–1990*. Columbus: Ohio State University Press, 1993.

ACTIVIST

Martinsson, Johanna. "#2: Activism Versus Advocacy." *People, Space, Deliberation* (blog). The World Bank, December 30, 2011. https://blogs.worldbank.org/publicsphere /activism-versus-advocacy.

ADOPTABLE

Goudreau, Kim. "My Family Background Information Made Up by Holt." *Holt Adoption Product* (blog), October 7, 2015. https://holtproduct.wordpress.com/2015/10/07 /my-family-background-information-made-up-by-holt/.

Hawes, Jennifer Berry. "After a Life of Tragedy, South Carolina Woman Places Hope in Finding a Lost Son." *Post and Courier* (Charleston, SC), January 28, 2018. https://www.postandcourier .com/features/after-a-life-of-tragedy-south-carolina-woman -places-hope/article_748b9420-fbcf-11e7-996e-4b16f20921d2 .html.

Lavandera, Ed, and Jeremy Harlan. "Police Officer Adopts Homeless Mother's Opioid-Addicted Newborn." CNN, December 3, 2017. http://www.cnn.com/2017/12/01/health

/police-officer-adopts-homeless-opioid-newborn-btc-beyond-the
-call-of-duty/index.html.

Overall, Michael. "One Year Later, Baby Veronica Case Still
Resonates." *Tulsa World,* September 21, 2014. http://www
.tulsaworld.com/news/courts/one-year-later-baby
-veronica-case-still-resonates/article_2b85eeef-72c5-50cb-b3e8
-74f9dfe7355e.html.

Robb, Amanda. "Why One Mother Gave Back Her Adopted
Son." *Good Housekeeping,* November 2, 2015. http://www
.goodhousekeeping.com/life/parenting/tips/a19902
/giving-up-adopted-children/. *(Author's note: It's offensive to this
adoptee that the article is listed under "parenting tips.")*

ADOPTION

The Free Dictionary. s.v. "adoption." Accessed March 27, 2018.
https://legal-dictionary.thefreedictionary.com/adoption.

"Adoption: An Overview." Legal Information Institute, Cornell
Law School. Accessed March 27, 2018. https://www.law.cornell
.edu/wex/adoption.

"Adoption Procedures." Nolo. Accessed March 27, 2018. https://
www.nolo.com/legal-encyclopedia/adoption-procedures-30201
.html.

Carney, Eliza Newlin. "The Truth About Domestic Infant
Adoption." Adoptive Families. Accessed March 27,

2018. https://www.adoptivefamilies.com/how-to-adopt
/domestic-adoption-myths-and-truths/.

"How Much Does It Cost to Adopt a Child?" American Adoptions.
Accessed March 27, 2018. http://www.americanadoptions.com
/adopt/why_does_private_adoption_cost_so_much_money.

"How Soon after Birth Do Adoptive Parents Take the Baby?"
Adoption Network Law Center. Accessed March 27, 2018.
https://adoptionnetwork.com/how-soon-after-birth-do
-adoptive-parents-take-the-baby.

Lunchik, Paisley, RVT. "What Is the Best Age to Send Puppies
to Their New Homes?" American Kennel Club, June 10, 2018.
http://www.akc.org/content/dog-breeding/articles/best-age
-send-puppies-to-new-homes/.

"Off and Running: Fact Sheet." PBS. Accessed March 27, 2018.
http://www.pbs.org/pov/offandrunning/fact-sheet/.

"Planning for Adoption: Knowing the Costs and Resources."
Child Welfare Information Gateway, November 2016. https://
www.childwelfare.gov/pubpdfs/s_costs.pdf.

"Six Words: Black Babies Cost Less to Adopt." NPR, June 27,
2013. https://www.npr.org/2013/06/27/195967886/six-words
-black-babies-cost-less-to-adopt.

"What Is the Cost of Adoption from Foster Care?" AdoptUSKids.
Accessed March 27, 2018. https://www.adoptuskids.org
/adoption-and-foster-care/overview/what-does-it-cost.

ADVERSE CHILDHOOD EXPERIENCES

"Adverse Childhood Experiences." SAMHSA. Last modified September 5, 2017. https://www.samhsa.gov/capt/practicing -effective-prevention/prevention-behavioral-health /adverse-childhood-experiences.

"Got Your ACE Score?" ACEs Too High. Accessed March 27, 2018. https://acestoohigh.com/got-your-ace-score/.

White, Christine Cissy. "Putting Resilience and Resilience Surveys Under the Microscope." ACEs Too High, February 5, 2017. https://acestoohigh.com/2017/02/05/__trashed-4/.

AFFAIR

Palmer, Caitríona. *An Affair with My Mother*. Dublin: Penguin Ireland, 2016.

AMBIGUOUS

Boss, Pauline. "The Trauma and Complicated Grief of Ambiguous Loss." *Pastoral Psychology* 59 (2010): 137–145. doi:10.1007/s11089-009-0264-0. http://www.bfomidwest.org /wp-content/uploads/2014/03/The-Trauma-and-Complicated -Grief-of-Ambiguous-Loss-Boss-2010.pdf.

ANGER

Kassinove, Howard, PhD. "How to recognize and deal with anger." American Psychological Association. Accessed March 27, 2018. http://www.apa.org/helpcenter/recognize-anger.aspx.

Mills, Harry, PhD. "Psychology of Anger." MentalHelp.net. Last modified December 22, 2015. https://www.mentalhelp.net/articles/psychology-of-anger/.

Seltzer, Leon F., PhD. "What Your Anger May Be Hiding." _Evolution of the Self_ (blog), _Psychology Today_, July 11, 2008. https://www.psychologytoday.com/blog/evolution-the-self/200807/what-your-anger-may-be-hiding.

ATTACHMENT

"Attachment Theory." Psychologist World. Accessed March 28, 2018. https://www.psychologistworld.com/developmental/attachment-theory.

Boris, Neil W., MD, and Charles H. Zeanah, MD. "Practice Parameter for the Assessment and Treatment of Children and Adolescents with Reactive Attachment Disorder of Infancy and Early Childhood." _Journal of the American Academy of Child & Adolescent Psychiatry_ 44, no. 11 (November 2005): 1206–1219. doi:10.1097/01.chi.0000177056.41655.ce. http://www.jaacap.com/article/S0890-8567(09)62229-2/fulltext.

Firestone, Lisa, PhD. "How Your Attachment Style Impacts Your Relationship." *Compassion Matters* (blog), *Psychology Today,* July 30, 2013. https://www.psychologytoday.com/blog/compassion-matters/201307/how-your-attachment-style-impacts-your-relationship.

Fraley, R. Chris. "A Brief Overview of Adult Attachment Theory and Research." University of Illinois at Urbana-Champaign, Psychology Department, 2010. https://internal.psychology.illinois.edu/~rcfraley/attachment.htm.

"Harry Harlow." PBS. Accessed March 27, 2018. http://www.pbs.org/wgbh/aso/databank/entries/bhharl.html.

McLeod, Saul. "Attachment Theory." Simply Psychology, 2009. https://www.simplypsychology.org/attachment.html.

McLeod, Saul. "Mary Ainsworth." Simply Psychology. Last modified 2016. https://www.simplypsychology.org/mary-ainsworth.html.

Mercer, Jean, PhD. "Coercive Restraint Therapies: A Dangerous Alternative Mental Health Intervention." Medscape, 2005. https://www.medscape.com/viewarticle/508956.

"Reactive Attachment Disorder." Mayo Clinic. Accessed March 28, 2018. https://www.mayoclinic.org/diseases-conditions/reactive-attachment-disorder/symptoms-causes/syc-20352939.

"Reactive Attachment Disorder." *Psychology Today.* Last modified March 5, 2018. https://www.psychologytoday.com/conditions/reactive-attachment-disorder.

Schechter, Daniel S., MD, and Erica Willheim, PhD. "Disturbances of Attachment and Parental Psychopathology in Early Childhood." *PMC* (July 1, 2010). doi:10.1016 /j.chc.2009.03.001. https://www.ncbi.nlm.nih.gov/pmc /articles/PMC2690512/.

BABY SCOOP ERA

"Adolescent Sexual and Reproductive Health in the United States." Guttmacher Institute. Accessed March 28, 2018. https://www.guttmacher.org/fact-sheet/american-teens -sexual-and-reproductive-health.

Chandra, Anjani, PhD, Penelope Maza, PhD, and Christine Bachrach, PhD. "Adoption, Adoption Seeking, and Relinquishment for Adoption in the United States." *Advance Data,* no. 306, Centers for Disease Control and Prevention, May 11, 1999. https://www.cdc.gov/nchs/data/ad/ad306.pdf.

Cunningham, Shelby. "Smashed by Adoption (Baby Scoop Era)." Origins Australia (Forced Adoption Support Network), May 26, 2010. http://www.originsnsw.com/id43.html.

Hasstedt, Kinsey, and Heather Boonstra. "Taking Stock of Year One of the Trump Administration's Harmful Agenda against Reproductive Health and Rights." *Rewire.News,* January 18, 2018. https://rewire.news/article/2018/01/18 /taking-stock-year-one-trump-administrations-harmful-agenda -reproductive-health-rights/.

Joyce, Kathryn. "'Philomena' Reminds Us That the 'Baby Scoop Era' Affected Millions." *Rewire.News,* February 3, 2014. https://rewire.news/article/2014/02/03/philomena -reminds-us-baby-scoop-era-affected-millions/.

Kliff, Sarah. "Charts: How Roe v. Wade Changed Abortion Rights." *Washington Post,* January 22, 2013. https:// www.washingtonpost.com/news/wonk/wp/2013/01/22 /charts-how-roe-v-wade-changed-abortion-rights/.

Rubio, Julie Hanlon. "Pope Francis Has an Unusually Positive View of Sex." *Washington Post,* April 12, 2016. https:// www.washingtonpost.com/news/acts-of-faith/wp/2016/04 /12/pope-francis-has-an-unusually-positive-view-of-sex/.

Saxon, Wolfgang. "Joseph H. Reid, 78, Director of League on Child Welfare." *New York Times,* November 24, 1994. http:// www.nytimes.com/1994/11/24/obituaries/joseph-h-reid-78 -director-of-league-on-child-welfare.html.

"Trends in U.S. Adoptions: 2008–2012." Child Welfare Information Gateway, January 2016. https://www.childwelfare .gov/pubPDFs/adopted0812.pdf.

"What Was the 'Baby Scoop Era'?" The Baby Scoop Era Research Initiative. Accessed March 28, 2018. http://babyscoopera.com /home/what-was-the-baby-scoop-era/.

CHOICE

Bailey, Martha J., Melanie Guldi, Allison Davido, and Erin Buzuvis. "Early Legal Access: Laws and Policies Governing Contraceptive Access, 1960–1980." University of Michigan, August 2011. http://www-personal.umich.edu/~baileymj /ELA_laws.pdf.

Thompson, Kirsten M. J. "A Brief History of Birth Control in the U.S." Our Bodies Ourselves, December 14, 2013. https://www.ourbodiesourselves.org/health-info /a-brief-history-of-birth-control/.

DNA

"Genetics Overview." *National Geographic*. Accessed March 28, 2018. https://genographic.nationalgeographic.com /genetics-overview/.

Khan, Razib. "Which Grandparent Are You Most Related To?" *Slate,* October 18, 2013. http://www.slate.com/articles/health _and_science/human_genome/2013/10/analyze_your_child_s _dna_which_grandparents_are_most_genetically_related.html.

Swayne, Anna. "Understanding Patterns of Inheritance: Where Did My DNA Come From? (And Why It Matters)." *Ancestry Blog* (blog), Ancestry, March 5, 2014. https://blogs.ancestry.com /ancestry/2014/03/05/understanding-patterns-of-inheirtance -where-did-my-dna-come-from-and-why-it-matters/.

"Where Do Your Genes Come From?" 23andMe. Accessed March 28, 2018. https://www.23andme.com/gen101/origins/.

FAMILY TREE

Edwards, Haley Sweetland. "6 of the Oldest Trees in the World." *Mental Floss,* April 26, 2014. http://mentalfloss.com /article/29879/6-oldest-trees-world.

"How Trees Grow." Texas A&M Forest Service. Accessed March 28, 2018. http://texastreeid.tamu.edu/content/howTreesGrow/.

Tu, Chau. "Earth's Biggest Living Thing Might Be a Tree with Thousands of Clones." PRI (Public Radio International), May 5, 2015. https://www.pri.org/stories/2015-05-05 /earths-biggest-living-thing-might-be-tree-thousands-clones.

Waller, Sarah. "Scientists Peek into the Hidden World of Tree Roots." KUOW (Seattle), May 30, 2013. http://kuow.org/post /scientists-peek-hidden-world-tree-roots.

HOME

McAndrew, Frank T., PhD. "Home Is Where the Heart Is, but Where Is 'Home'?" *Out of the Ooze* (blog), *Psychology Today,* August 3, 2015. https://www.psychologytoday.com /blog/out-the-ooze/201508/home-is-where-the-heart-is-where -is-home.

Raab, Diana, PhD. "Where Is Your Home?" *The Empowerment Diary* (blog), *Psychology Today,* June 27, 2017. https://www.psychologytoday.com/blog/the-empowerment-diary/201706/where-is-your-home.

ILLEGITIMATE

Brumberg, H. L., D. Dozor, and S. G. Golombek. "History of the Birth Certificate: From Inception to the Future of Electronic Data." *Journal of Perinatology* 32 (2012): 407–411. doi:10.1038/jp.2012.3. https://www.nature.com/articles/jp20123.

Corbin, Judge R. Thomas, and Rana Holz. "Distinguishing Legitimacy from Paternity: Has Legitimacy Become a Label Without Substance Under Flo." *Florida Bar Journal* 73, no. 1 (January 1999): 57. Last modified February 10, 2012. https://www.floridabar.org/news/tfb-journal/?durl=%2FDIVCOM%2FJN%2FJNJournal01.nsf%2FAuthor%2F77E5D005C9FB72A585256ADB005D6235.

DePasquale, Sara. "Legitimation vs. Paternity: What's the Difference?" *On the Civil Side* (blog), UNC School of Government. Last modified October 24, 2016. https://civil.sog.unc.edu/legitimation-versus-paternity-whats-the-difference/.

Ro, Christine. "A Birth Certificate Is a Person's First Possession." *Atlantic,* December 10, 2017. https://www.theatlantic.com/technology/archive/2017/12/a-birth-certificate-is-a-persons-first-possession/547970/.

"Rules Regarding Natural Legitimate Parent-Child Relationship."
Social Security Administration, June 26, 2012. https://secure.ssa
.gov/poms.nsf/lnx/0200306010.

"Legal Definition of 'Father' by State." FindLaw. Accessed March
28, 2018. http://family.findlaw.com/paternity/legal-definition
-of-father-by-state.html.

Opinion No. H-1078 Re: Duties of a hospital district in
preparation of birth certificates. John L. Hill, Attorney General
of Texas, October 26, 1977. https://www.texasattorneygeneral
.gov/opinions/opinions/45hill/op/1977/htm/jh1078.htm.

LOST

J. R. R. Tolkien. *The Fellowship of the Ring: Being the First Part of
The Lord of the Rings*. New York: Ballantine Books, 2012. *(Quote:
"Not all those who wander are lost.")*

MATERNITY HOME

Beyerstein, Lindsay E. "Sent Away: A New Look at Maternity
Group Homes." *Rewire.News,* June 21, 2007. https://rewire
.news/article/2007/06/21/sent-away-a-new-look-at-maternity
-group-homes/.

"Booth Memorial Hospital." *Encyclopedia of Cleveland History,*
Case Western Reserve University. Accessed March 28, 2018.
https://case.edu/ech/articles/b/booth-memorial-hospital/.

Mansnerus, Laura. "Community; No Shame but Plenty of Need at Home for Unwed Mothers." *New York Times,* February 15, 1998. http://www.nytimes.com/1998/02/15/nyregion /community-no-shame-but-plenty-of-need-at-home-for-unwed -mothers.html.

ORIGINAL BIRTH CERTIFICATE

"For the Records II: An Examination of the History and Impact of Adult Adoptee Access to Original Birth Certificates." Evan B. Donaldson Adoption Institute, July 2010. https://www .adoptioninstitute.org/wp-content/uploads/2013/12 /7_14_2010_ForTheRecordsII.pdf.

ORPHAN

Dherbeys, Agnes. "Broken Bloodlines: A South Korean Adoptee Tells the Mothers' Tales." *Post Magazine (South China Morning Post)*, January 11, 2014. http://www.scmp.com/magazines /post-magazine/article/1401453/broken-bloodlines-south -korean-adoptee-tells-mothers-tales.

"Orphans." Unicef. Last modified June 16, 2017. https://www .unicef.org/media/media_45279.html.

"Orphan Statistics Explained." The Schuster Institute for Investigative Journalism, Brandeis University. Last modified February 23, 2011. https://www.brandeis.edu/investigate /adoption/orphan-statistics.html#orphans.

Van Doore, Kate. "The Business of Orphanages: Where Do 'Orphans' Come From?" *The Conversation,* March 9, 2015. http://theconversation.com/the-business-of-orphanages-where -do-orphans-come-from-38485.

PRIMAL WOUND

Verrier, Nancy Newton. *The Primal Wound.* Baltimore: Gateway Press, 1993.

"Baby Sea Turtles." SEE Turtles. Accessed March 28, 2018. http://www.seeturtles.org/baby-turtles/.

Digitale, Erin. "Mom's Voice Activates Many Different Regions in Children's Brains." *Stanford Medicine News,* May 16, 2016. https://med.stanford.edu/news/all-news/2016/05/moms-voice -activates-different-regions-in-children-brains.html.

Fehlhaber, Kate. "How a Mother's Voice Shapes Her Baby's Developing Brain." *Aeon,* October 6, 2016. https://aeon.co /ideas/how-a-mother-s-voice-shapes-her-baby-s-developing-brain.

Lang, Kristina Cawthon. "Chimpanzee: Pan Troglodytes." Primate Info Net, Library Information Service, National Primate Research Center, University of Wisconsin–Madison. Last modified April 13, 2006. http://pin.primate.wisc.edu /factsheets/entry/chimpanzee/behav.

McCarthy, Laura Flynn. "What Babies Learn in the Womb." Parenting. Accessed March 28, 2018. http://www.parenting .com/article/what-babies-learn-in-the-womb.

"Mom's Voice Plays Special Role in Activating Newborn's Brain." *Science Daily,* December 17, 2010. https://www.sciencedaily .com/releases/2010/12/101215195234.htm.

Querleu, D., C. Lefebvre, M. Titran, X. Renard, M. Morillion, and G. Crepin. "Reaction of the Newborn Infant Less Than 2 Hours after Birth to the Maternal Voice." Abstract. *Journal de gynécologie, obstétrique et biologie de la reproduction* 132, no. 2 (1984): 125–34. https://www.ncbi.nlm.nih.gov /pubmed/6736589.

PUTATIVE FATHER

Fetrow, Karen L. "Unwed Fathers' Rights Regarding Infant Adoption." *Musings of the Lame* (blog), May 12, 2014. http:// www.adoptionbirthmothers.com/unwed-fathers-rights-regarding -infant-adoption/.

Lewin, Tamar. "Unwed Fathers Fight for Babies Placed for Adoption by Mothers." *New York Times,* March 19, 2006. http:// www.nytimes.com/2006/03/19/us/unwed-fathers-fight-for -babies-placed-for-adoption-by-mothers.html.

"Putative Father Registry." Academy of Adoption and Assisted Reproduction Attorneys. Accessed March 28, 2018. http://www.adoptionattorneys.org/aaaa/birth-parents/putative-father-registry.

"The Rights of Unmarried Fathers." Child Welfare Information Gateway, January 2014. https://www.childwelfare.gov/pubPDFs/putative.pdf.

REDACT

In Ohio, a law went into effect in March 2015 allowing access to original birth certificates (OBCs) for adoptees born between 1964 and 1996 (adoptees born outside this range already had access to their OBCs). The law allowed birth parents until March 19, 2015, to request that their names be redacted from copies of birth certificates seen by the children they relinquished for adoption. Of the approximately 400,000 adoptee birth records impacted, only 259 redaction requests were received (0.06 percent of the total). Some of the adoptees who applied earliest for their OBCs and whose parents requested their names be redacted received documents with much more blacked out than just their parent's name. Officials processing the requests took it upon themselves to redact any bit of information they thought might lead to identification of a parent, including the adopted person's own name. After receiving complaints, the Ohio Department of Health reviewed the new law's language, and reissued those birth certificates with only the birth parent's name redacted, as was the law's intent.

"Adult Adoptee & Birthparent Hub: Search and Reunion— Frequently Asked Questions." Adoption Network Cleveland. Accessed May 15, 2018. https://adoptionnetwork-org .presencehost.net/service-areas/adult-adoptee-birthparent-hub /questions.html#content_ad98cfdc6863f2bc381a438530b8d02e _item_10000136.

Luce, Gregory D. "Ohio." Adoptee Rights Law. Last modified June 3, 2017. https://adopteerightslaw.com/ohio-obc/.

"Ohio to Reissue Some Adoptees' Newly Unsealed Birth Records." *News-Herald* (Willoughby, OH), September 23, 2015. http://www.news-herald.com/article/HR/20150923 /NEWS/150929818.

SIN

"2 Genesis." *New American Bible, Revised Edition.* United States Conference of Catholic Bishops. Accessed March 28, 2018. http://www.usccb.org/bible/genesis/2.

2015–16 Student Handbook & Calendar of Events. Marian Catholic High School (Chicago Heights, IL). Accessed March 28, 2018. http://www.marianchs.com/pdf/2015-2016 -Handbook.pdf.

2017–18 Student Handbook. Kapaun Mt. Carmel Catholic High School (Wichita, KS). Accessed March 28, 2018. http://www .kapaun.org/academics/student-handbook/file.

Student Handbook 2017–18. Regis Jesuit (Aurora, CO). Accessed March 28, 2018. https://www.regisjesuit.com/file /StudentHandbook.pdf.

SURRENDER

The form my mother signed that made me adoptable was titled "Permanent Surrender of Child." From the form:

> . . . the undersigned will abide by the rules and regulations of the certified institution or organization, board or department, not to communicate with said child, or induce him/her to leave the institution or family with whom he/she might be placed, and to sever all connections with said child . . .

UNPLANNED/UNEXPECTED CHILD

Gajanan, Mahita. "The Cost of Raising a Child Jumps to $233,610." *Money*, January 9, 2017. http://time.com/money/4629700 /child-raising-cost-department-of-agriculture-report/.

O'Brien, Elizabeth and Pratheek Rebala. "Find Out How Much It Costs to Give Birth in Every State." *Money*, October 30, 2017. http://time.com/money/4995922/how-much-costs -give-birth-state/.

ACKNOWLEDGMENTS

Thanks to Deborah Steinberg and Madeleine Vasaly for helping me shape and polish these words.

Thanks to everyone at Lost Daughters and to everyone in the adoption community I've met both in person and online. A great deal of what I now understand about the adoption world and my place in it stems from the interactions I've had with all of you. I am grateful to have received this gift of knowledge, and I am committed to continue learning. Thanks especially to Amanda Woolston for creating a space specifically for adopted women and for allowing me to participate in that space.

Although this book was not yet conceived then, I am grateful to my professors and fellow students in the MAPW program at Kennesaw State University for their feedback on the numerous adoption-related pieces in multiple genres that I workshopped while there.

Thanks to Keep St. Pete Lit instructors Gloria Muñoz, Lenore Myka, and Sabrina Dalla Valle for opening me up to new explorations in my writing via their workshops.

Thanks to Adoption Network Cleveland for helping me reconnect with my birth family. Thanks to Betsie Norris for tirelessly supporting Ohio adoptees, including this one.

Thank you every day, John, for never-ending support. I love you.

INDEX

abortion *30*

activist *63*

adoptable *45*

adoptee *65*

adoption *79*

adverse childhood experiences (ACEs) *75*

affair *71*

ambiguous *33*

anger *61*

attachment *77*

baby *6*

Baby Scoop Era *58*

best interests of the child *17*

birth family *53*

child *13*

choice *83*

DNA *26*

family tree *11*

first *55*

geometry *51*

grief *73*

home *49*

illegitimate *64*

kin *47*

lost *39*

maternity home *15*

mirror *67*

name *8*

native *12*

normal *19*

original birth certificate (OBC) *37*

orphan *21*

parent *81*

placement *14*

primal wound *35*

putative father *24*

redact *28*

relinquish *42*

reunion *52*

secret *70*

sin *3*

surrender *41*

termination of parental rights *43*

unplanned/unexpected child *56*

welfare *69*

CPSIA information can be obtained
at www.ICGtesting.com
Printed in the USA
BVHW071219180321
602885BV00008B/899